The Fulfilment of the Prophetic Scriptures Pertaining to The Christ in His Second Advent

Written by:

G. Michael Cordeiro

First version: 2009
Second edition: 2013

ISBN: 978-1-300-78523-1

Part proceeds of this book will be donated to
The Shashamane Trust Fund

Co-edited by: Jason T. Dollemont
Book design and layout: Jocelyne Lapointe

Contents

Ackowledgements...A

Preface..B

Dedications...C

The Second Advent of The Christ...1

The birth of Ras Tafari Mekonnen.......................................5

The Prophesies and their fulfillments...................................6

The Coronation of: the King of Kings, Lord of Lords,.............11
Conquering Lion of the Tribe of Judah

The War against the King of Kings, Elect of God....................21

Accolades and accomplishments..24

Medals, Titles and Decorations...37

Utterances of His Imperial Majesty......................................41

Tribes of Israel...46

Other important figures..47

The Fathers' prayer in Ge'ez, Amharic and English................48

Bibliography..54

Glosary..55

Acknowledgments

Many thanks to everyone who provided their help and support in the making of this holy book, although I could not list everyone, thank you all the same.

Special thanks go out to: Christine Graystone for the insightful proofreading of the manuscript with detailed remarks and strict adherence to consistency; Jason Dollemont for co-editing the manuscript and his enthusiasm for spreading The Good Word; Glenford Samuels (aka. Ras Digital) for being a conscious-aware-witness unto the revelation of The Christ in His Second Advent, and the Revelation of The Precious Name of The Father in His Holy Elect One: Germawi Qedamawi Haile Sellassie; and also to Natty B at Trejah-Isle Records for being the first venue to distribute this book in Canada and for encouraging me to continue on with the book.

I'd also like to thank you, the reader, for taking interest in seeking H.I.M. and suggest that this book be read with a bible in hand, so that you may review the scriptures mentioned herein to over-stand them in their full context.

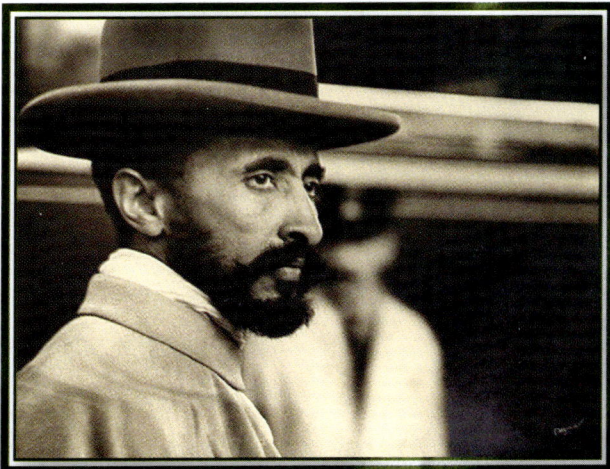

Preface

Having been raised a Catholic, it wasn't until my early teens when I became conscious of myself and received the Spirit of the Almighty.

I remember listening to Bob Marley for the first time and I was moved by the lyrics and messages he was singing about. My older sister was working at a music store at that time and she used to bring home different types of music for us to listen to. The first time that I had heard Bob's music, I knew his music was radically different than any other types of music that I had been exposed to. Bob's music was mystical and it had meaning to it.

He sang about peace, love and unity amongst all peoples. Also about the oppression of poor people in this world and the Redemption of (Wo)Man by the Revelation of That Divine and Precious Name of:

The Father-of-Creation,
as revealed in HIS Christ,
The Holy Elect One of Israel,
King of Kings, Lord of Lords,
The Conquering Lion of the Tribe of Judah:
Germawi Atse' Qedamawi Haile Sellassie
(His Imperial Majesty Emperor Haile Sellassie 1st).

When I had come into the realization of this divine revelation, from then on, I began to seek and praise The Father in HIS Precious and Perfect name: Germawi Qedamawi Haile Sellassie (The One and only Might of The Holy Tri-unity).

I in I give thanks and praises in the name of The Most High:
Germawi Qedamawi Haile Sellassie

B

Dedications

Greetings in the name of H.I.M. Ras Tafari, Germawi Qedamawi Haile Sellassie, Conquering Lion of the Tribe of Judah. Elect of GOD and True Light of The World.

I would like to dedicate this book to GOD Almighty, my daughter Terrylynn, and to all the fatherless and motherless children of this world, for giving me the inspirations to be able to achieve this monumental undertaking. To all faithful Rastafarians throughout this world who have been oppressed and persecuted by Babylon, keep the faith my brothers and sisters, for the time is HERE and NOW.

The Second Advent of the Christ

" I am the root and the offspring of David,
and the bright and morning star."
Revelations 22:16

It is with great joy that I share the following biblical prophesies of the second advent of The Christ and how they have been fulfilled by only one: Germawi Qedamawi Haile Sellassie.

The Christ tells us of the signs if His return, in the flesh.

Luke 24:44. "Christ said, "...all things must be fulfilled, which were written in the Law of Moses and in the prophets and in the psalms, concerning me.""

Luke 1:32 "He shall be great, and shall be called the Son of the Highest: and the Lord God shall give unto him the throne of his father David."

Mathew 24:

3 "As Jesus sat down upon the mount of Olives, the disciples came unto him saying, Tell us, when shall these things be? What shall be the sign of thy coming, and of the end of the world?"

4 "and Jesus answered and said unto them, "Take heed that no man deceive you."

5 "For many shall come in my name, saying, I am Christ; and shall deceive many."

29 "Immediately after the tribulation of those days shall the sun be darkened, and the moon shall not give her light, and the stars shall fall from heaven, and the powers of the heavens shall be shaken." (See also Isaiah 13:10, Joel 2:10-11 and Zephaniah 1:15)

30 "And then shall the sign of the Son of man in heaven: and than shall all the tribes of the earth mourn, and they shall see the Son of man coming in the clouds of heaven with power and great glory." (See also Mark 13:26)

33 "Christ said. "So likewise ye, when ye shall see all these things, know that it is near, even at the doors.""

Matthew 25:31 "When the Son of man shall come in his glory, and all the holy Angels with him, than shall he sit upon the throne of his glory."

Revelation 1:

7 "Behold, he cometh with clouds; and every eye shall see him, and they also which pierced him: and all kindreds of the earth shall wail because of him. Even so, Amen."

8 ""I am Alpha and Omega, the Beginning and the Ending, saith the Lord, which is, and which was, and which is to come, the Almighty.""

2

Revelations 5:

1 "And I saw in the right hand of him that sat on the throne a book written within and on the backside, sealed with seven seals."

2 "And I saw a strong angel proclaiming with a loud voice, Who is worthy to open the book, and to loose the seals thereof?"

3 "And no man in heaven, nor in earth, neither under the earth, was able to open the book, neither to look thereon."

4 "And I wept much, because no man was found worthy to open and to read the book, neither to look thereon."

5 "And one of the elders saith unto me, Weep not: behold, the Lion of the tribe of Judah, the Root of David, hath prevailed to open the book, and to loose the seven seals thereof."

6 "And I beheld, and, lo, in the midst of the throne and of the four beasts, and in the midst of the elders, stood a Lamb as it had been slain…"

12 "…Worthy is the Lamb that was slain to receive power, and riches, and wisdom, and strength, and honour, and glory, and blessing."

13 "And every creature which is in heaven, and on the earth, and under the earth, and such as are in the sea, and all that are in them, heard I saying, Blessing, and honour, and glory, and power, be unto him that sitteth upon the throne, and unto the Lamb for ever and ever."

14 "And the four beasts said, Amen. And the four and twenty elders fell down and worshipped him that liveth for ever and ever."

Revelations 19:

7 "Let us be glad and rejoice, and give honour to him: for the marriage of the Lamb is come, and his wife hath made herself ready."

8 "And to her was granted that she should be arrayed in fine linen, clean and white: for the fine linen is the righteousness of saints."

9 "And he saith unto me, Write, Blessed are they which are called unto the marriage supper of the Lamb. And he saith unto me, These are the true sayings of God."

10 "And I fell at his feet to worship him. And he said unto me, See thou do it not: I am thy fellowservant, and of thy brethren that have the testimony of Jesus: worship God: for the testimony of Jesus is the spirit of prophecy."

11 "And I saw heaven opened, and behold a white horse; and he that sat upon him was called Faithful and True, and in righteousness he doth judge and make war."

12 "His eyes were as a flame of fire, and on his head were many crowns; and he had a name written, that no man knew, but he himself."

13 "And he was clothed with a vesture dipped in blood: and his name is called The Word of God."

14 "And the armies which were in heaven followed him upon white horses, clothed in fine linen, white and clean."

15 "And out of his mouth goeth a sharp sword, that with it he should smite the nations: and he shall rule them with a rod of iron: and he treadeth the winepress of the fierceness and wrath of Almighty God."

16 "And he hath on his vesture and on his thigh a name written, King Of Kings, And Lord Of Lords."

The Birth of Tafari Mekonnen

The birth of Tafari (alt. spl. Teferi) Mekonnen, The One to bear The Name: Germawi Qedamawi Haile Sellassie, had been foretold by astrologers and chaplains that the celestial bodies of Neptune and Pluto, would cross each other in July 1892, which had started moving towards each other some 493 years earlier in 1399.

The 19th day of May, 1780, is known in History as the "Dark Day", because an unexplained Darkness on this day covered a large portion of the New World. The sun was darkened and the moon did not give any light on the night following this "Dark Day". (See also Isaiah 13:10-13)

On July 23rd 1892, in the year of John, a boy child was born in the village of Ejarsa, Goro, outside the city of Harrar in Ethiopia, whose birth name is Tafari Mekonnen.

Psalm 68:31 "..Ethiopia shall soon stretch out her hands to God."

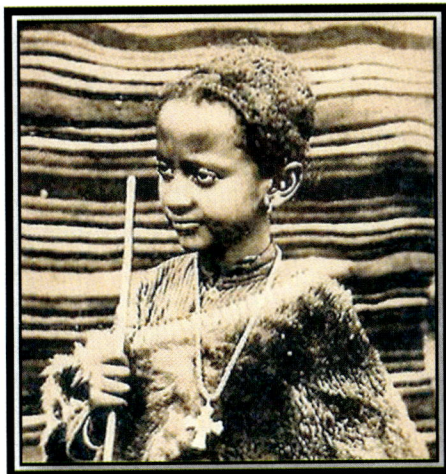

The Prophesies and their Fulfillments

"I will make mention of Rahab
and Babylon to them that know me;
behold Philistia, and Tyre, with
E-thi-opi-a: this man was born there"
Psalm 87:4

On May 19, 1780, the Sun and the Moon were darkened and it is well known in history as "The Dark Day". (See also Matthew 24:27, 29 and 33)

In the year 1798, the pope Pius VI was kidnapped by Napoleon Bonaparte and exiled in Valence, France. This event had ended the 1260 years of papal supremacy and Rome's rule of Europe which began in A.D. 538. Forcing "the beast" the devil to flee into the wilderness after 1260 years of Satan's rule on Earth. Thus fulfilling another of the prophecies of the returning of Christ in his 2nd advent.

Psalm 87:

4 "The Lord said "I will make mention of Rahab and Babylon to them that know me: Behold Philistia and Tyre, with Ethiopia; "This man was born there."

5 "And of Zion it shall be said, This and that man was born in her: and The Highest Himself shall establish her."

Permit us to analyze the sentence "**This man** was born there." Now the subject of this sentence is, this man. The subject of the Psalm is **the Lord**. So The Lord is the subject of the Psalm and this man is the subject of the sentence. **Therefore**, by substitution it would read: The Lord was born there.

6

Now, "**there**" is the object in this sentence and functioning as a demonstrative Pronoun of a place. The grammatical logic to determine whether the object, "there" refers to Phillstia, Tyre or Ethiopia, is revealed by the preposition "**with**". The preposition "with", indicates that Ethiopia is the Noun for the demonstrative object pronoun "there". **Therefore**, if we substitute "this man" for The Lord and "there" for Ethiopia, the sentence would read: The Lord was born in Ethiopia.

We know that the Christ, in His First Advent, was born in Bethlehem of Judae (See also Matthew 2:1).

Therefore, as in Psalm 87:4, The Lord was born in Ethiopia, so it must be the fulfillment of the Christ's Second Advent.

The stars fell on November 13, 1833, fulfilling another of the Saviours' prophecies of the nearness of His coming. (See also Matthew 24:27, 29, 30 and 33)

Isaiah 9:6 "For unto us a child is born, unto us a son is given: and the government shall be upon his shoulder: and his name shall be called Wonderful, Counsellor, The Mighty GOD, The Everlasting Father, The Prince of Peace."

Genesis 49:10 "The sceptre shall not depart from Judah, nor a lawgiver from between his feet, until Shiloh come; and unto him shall the gathering of the people be."

Psalm 76:1 "In Judah *is* God known: His name *is* great in Israel."

Hebrew 7:14 "For it is evident that our Lord sprang out of the tribe of Judah."

Germawi Qedamawi Haile Sellassie, is the 113th King of the Christian Empire and He is also the 225th in a direct bloodline of the Ethiopian monarch, Menelik 1st. Menelik 1st is the first of the Solomonic Emperors of Ethiopia and was the first born son of the Queen of Sheba (Ethiopia) and King Solomon, who is the son of king David of Israel, who is the son of Jesse of the Tribe of Judah. Therefore, Germawi Qedamawi Haile Sellassie is from the tribe of Judah.

Revelation 22:16 "Christ said. "...I am the root and the offspring of David.""

Verily, He is the root of all things: The True and Living Christ is The Root, for, He Is, before the creation of the world, even prior to the creation of all creation.

Verily, He is the offspring of David: He has chosen for Himself a specific people (Israel), and a specific tribe (Judah), with a specific lineage (Jesse, David, Solomon, Menelik) which He chose to be born through.

The fulfillment of these and the other prophesies would all serve as witness to His Revelation, so that He would have no need to claim that He is The Christ.

Those who know the Son, shall know The Father, for they are One in the same.

John 14:9 """...Whoever has seen me has seen The Father.""""

11 """...Believe me that I am in the Father, and the Father in me: or else believe me for the very works' sake.""""

Revelation 1:14 "His head and his hairs were white like wool..."

Men of dark complexion naturaly have wooly, sheep-like hair and The Christ, as a Nazarite, is wearing locks. Germawi Qedamawi Haile Sellassie has white wooly hair.

Revelation 1:15 "And his feet like fine brass, as if they burned in a furnace..."

Brass has the complexion of a man with dark skin and in fact when looking at Germawi Qedamawi Haile Sellassie, one can see He has the complexion of all people, from all nations, in one.

Revelation 19: 7 "Let us be glad and rejoice, and give honor to him: for the marriage of the Lamb is come, and his wife hath made herself ready."

Whereas, the Lamb is The Christ and the wife is Ethiopia.

Isaiah 53:10 "...he shall see his seed..."

In this sentence, he, is the pronoun for Christ and the object pronoun, seed, means children. Therefore, He shall see His seed meaning The Christ shall see His children in His Second Advent. Germawi Qedamawi Haile Sellassie begot six children, three boys and three girls.

1st John 4: 2 "Hereby know ye the Spirit of God: Every spirit that confesseth that Jesus Christ is come in the flesh is of God:" 3: "And every spirit that confesseth not that Jesus Christ is come in the flesh is not of God; and this is that spirit of antichrist, whereof ye have heard that it should come; and even now already is it in the world."

Look for Christ anytime in the flesh after November 13, 1833, because the falling of the stars fulfilled the prophecy which pertains to the nearness of The Christ's Second Advent. (Matthew 24:29)

Acts 2:

29 "Men and bretheren, let me freely speak to you of the patriarch David…"

30 "Therefore being a prophet, and knowing that God had sworn with an oath to him, that of the fruit of his loins, according to the flesh, he would raise up Christ to sit on his throne."

The Christ, in His First Advent, did not sit on King David's throne. This prophecy is now fulfilled.

The Christ states in Luke 24: 44. ""…all things must be fulfilled, which were written in the law of Moses, and in the prophets, and in the psalms, concerning me.""

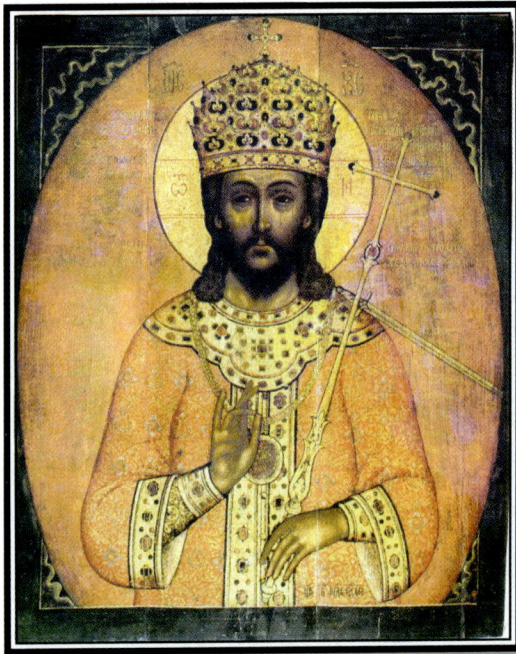

The Coronation of:
King of Kings, Lord of Lords, Conquering Lion of the Tribe of Judah

Christ said he would have a new name.
(See Revelation 3: 12)

On November 2, 1930, Negus (King) Tafari Mekonnen is crowned with a triple crown (three crown's in one), the divine scepter and a golden globe of the Earth to signify HIS authority in the Earth as The Holy Elect One.

On that day it was revealed a new name: Germawi Atse' Qedamawi Haile Sellassie (Amharic), which translates to:

Amheric	English
Germawi	*His Imperial Majesty (H.I.M.)*
Atse'	*Emperor*
Qedamawi	*The One and only*
Haile	*Might (alt. trans.: Power)*
Sellassie (alt. sp.: Selassie)	*The Holy Tri-unity*

girmāwī ḳedāmāwī 'aṣē ḫayle śillāsē, mō'ā 'anbessā ze'imneggede yihudā niguse negest ze'ītyōp̣p̣yā, siyume 'igzī'a'bihēr

During this coronation, Germawi Qedamawi Haile Sellassie, prophetically acquired the following titles which were honourably given to H.I.M. The titles are Emperor of Ethiopia, King of Kings, Lord of Lords and Conquering Lion of the Tribe of Judah and The Elect of GOD. (See also Revelation 19: 16)

Therefore, in 1930, Germawi Qedamawi Haile Sellassie, did sit on King David's throne and thus, fulfilled Acts 2: 29-30, because he is the fruit of King David's loins, according to the flesh. Germawi Qedamawi Haile Sellassie descended from King David's son King Solomon and his mother, the Queen of Sheba.

The prophet Ezekiel said that during his vision of God, he saw a throne: As the appearance of the bow that is in the cloud in the day of rain, so was the appearance of the brightness round about. This was the appearance of the likeness of the glory of the Lord. (See Ezekiel 1:26-28 for further referrence)

Revelation 4: 3 "And He (Christ) that sat was to look upon like a Jasper and a Sardine stone: and there was a rainbow round about the throne, in sight like unto an Emerald."

Germawi Qedamawi Haile Sellassie, King of Kings, Lord of Lords, Conquering Lion of the Tribe of Judah and Emperor of Ethiopia does bear the rainbow round about his throne in the appearance of the brightness of the outstanding colours of the rainbow, RED-GOLD-GREEN, as these are the colours of Ethiopia.

The Lion of Judah (See Revelation 5: 5, Psalm 68:31, Psalm 76:1, Psalm 87:4, Psalm 99:3, Acts 2:29-30, Hebrew 7:14, and Jeremiah 14:2) and the Elect of God. (See Revelation 1:14-15)

The Father and The Christ are One, see John 14:8-11 where Christ said to Phillip, """...He that hath seen me, hath seen the Father... ...I am in the Father and the Father in me.""" Phillip was looking at The Messiah, who is attesting that He Himself is The Father. Therefore, The Father in His Christ is always in flesh, for He Himself formed man in His image and likeness. He further establishes His authority over life and death by His Resurection in the flesh and also that He shall return in Flesh.

His Holy Revelation is also His Holy Redemption, The Holy Redeemer comes to bring us into the rememberance that we are all One in Him, see: John 14:20 """At that day ye shall know that I am in my Father, and ye in me, and I in you."""

Germawi Qedamawi Haile Sellassie, is the only descendant of King David and King Solomon, according to the flesh, (See alos Acts 2:29-30) and the only man on earth who has fulfilled the prophecies pertaining to Jesus Christ's Seond Advent.

Germawi Qedamawi Haile Sellassie, is the only King of Kings; and Lord of Lords; and Conquering Lion of the Tribe of Judah, dwelling on the earth. (See also 1st Timothy 6:15)

It is important to note that there have been others who have held the title King of Kings, however, who else but H.I.M. have held all three titles as listed above?

*"The earth is the Lord's, and
the fullness thereof, the world,
and they that dwell therein."*
Psalms 24:1

It is internationally accepted that the Old Testament of the
Holy Bible was originally written in the Hebrew Language. The
Hebrew Language is read from right to left and there is no "J"
consonant in the Hebrew Language.

So therefore, allow us to examine the name Haile. When read
from right to left = Eliah. Eliah is the same name as Elijah because
there is no "J" consonant in the Hebrew alphabet. (See Webster's
Third New International Dictionary, page 61, for the Hebrew
alphabet)

Eliah means, whose God is Jehovah thus, Haile = Eliah =
whose God is Jehovah = The word of God. (See Revelation 19:13)

See also 1st Chronicle 8:27 as refrence for Eliah and Unger's
Bible Dictionary, page 300, but remember, Haile = Eliah = Elijah.

The name Sellassie possesses within it, in a jumbled
arrangement, the names Elias Ess. The identical letters which spell
Sellassie also, spell Elias Ess. Elias is the Greek-English version of
Elijah. (See Unger's Bible Dictionary, page 301, for Elias)

Since Elijah means my God is Jehovah and Elias = Elijah,
therefore, Elias means my God is Jehovah = The word of God.

Christ in His First Advent was called Elias by some. (See also
Matthew 16:14)

The name Ess in Yenisei, which is a language in Siberia, Russia means, the Creator of the world. The meaning of the name is the word of God. (See Revelation 19:13). To these Siberians, Ess created the first Humans out of clay. (See Genesis 2:7 and Dictionary of Gods and Goddesses Devils and Demons by Manfred Lurker, page 113, for Ess)

The name Qedamawi (One and only, also translated as the first or the one) is also relevant to Christ. It is, The word of God. (See Revelation 19:13 and 22:13, Christ said. "...I am the First.")

The name Haile Sellassie = Eliah Elias Ess First = The word of God (See Revelation 3:12, 17:11 and 19:13) Eliah Elias Ess are the esoteric, that is, metaphysical (beyond-physical) or inner (in-near) names existing with the names Haile Sellassie.

Again, reading from right to left Haile = Eliah and Sellassie consist of Elias Ess in a jumbled format, the identical letters which spell Sellassie.

Again, Haile Sellassie means the Power of The Triune (Tri-unity), that is, one person with three predominant characteristics.

The three prevalent qualities of Haile Sellassie are:[1] Life; [2] Lightning, and [3] Water.

Germawi Qedamawi Haile Sellassie represented the nineth pregnancy of his mother and the only infant born that lived beyond infancy. His characteristics of life became very pronounce after his mother Waiz Yeshimabeit was pregnant again after Him, but she died in child-birth.

The qualities of lightning and water were obvious because Ethiopia was experiencing a major drought throughout the country, but the birth of Ras Tafari was welcomed with lightning, thunder and a considerable down-pour of rain fell upon the land.

These three conspicuous features; Life, Lightning and Water exist within the name of Haile Sellassie, as Eliah Elias Ess. Haile Sellassie means The Power of the Tri-Unity.

It was previously mentioned that Ess means The Creator of The World. In addition Elias = Elijah and Eliah = Elijah because there is no "J" consonant in the Hebrew alphabet.

Esoterically or metaphysically, Eliah, Elias, Ess relates to the three conspicuous characteristics; Life, Lightning and Water. Remember, Eliah = Elijah, Elias = Elijah and Ess = The Creator.

Elijah's esoteric relation to [1] Life: he raises the widow's son. (1st Kings 17: 17-24) [2] lightning: he called down lightning (fire) from heaven. (2nd Kings 1:8-10) and [3] Water: he predicted no rain (1st Kings 17:1) and he caused water to fall as rain. (1st Kings 18:42-45).

There is no coincidence in esoterics or metaphysics. Conversely, there exists predetermination. Resultantly:

Haile Sellassie = The Might of the Tri-Unity = Eliah
Elias Ess = Life, Lightning, Water = Creator.

Amos 9:7 "Are ye not as children of the Ethiopians to me, O' children of Israel? Saith the Lord."

It is important to note that Israel was being compared to the Ethiopians. That is, before Israel existed, the Ethiopians were and still are the chosen people for the Creator.

The first land mentioned in the Holy Bible refers to Ethiopia (Cush) in the book of Genesis 2: 8-13. The Garden of Eden was within the land of Cush (Ethiopia). Havilah is a son of Cush, which is to say Ethiopia. (See also Genesis 10: 7, Unger's Bible Dictionary, page 327, for Ethiopia and page 231, for Cush).

Moses knew that the Ethiopians are the first righteous people for the Creator. As a consequence, Moses married an Ethiopian woman. It seems reasonable that a righteous man like Moses should marry a righteous woman. (See Numbers 12: 1)

Miriam and Aaron spoke against Moses because of the Ethiopian women whom he married. But, read Numbers 12:9-12 and see how the Creator chastised Miriam for her criticism against Moses. Moses knew of the special relationship between the Creator and Ethiopians before Israel existed.

Again, Amos 9:7 "Are ye not as children of the Ethiopians to me, O'children of Israel? Saith the Lord."

Remember, the Ethiopians are first and Israel second.

Psalm 87:4 "...with Ethiopia, This man was born there."

Isaiah 43:3 "For I am the Lord thy God.
The Holy One of Israel, thy Saviour: I gave Egypt for
thy ransom, E-thi-o'pi-a and Se'ba for thee."

Isaiah 9:7 "Of the increase of his government and Peace there shall be no end, upon the Throne of David, and upon his Kingdom."

Jeremiah 23:17 "For thus saith the Lord, "David shall never want a man to sit upon the Throne of the house of Israel."

Jeremiah 23:5 "Behold, the days come, saith the Lord, that I will raise to David a righteous branch and a king shall reign and prosper and shall execute Judgment and justice in the earth."

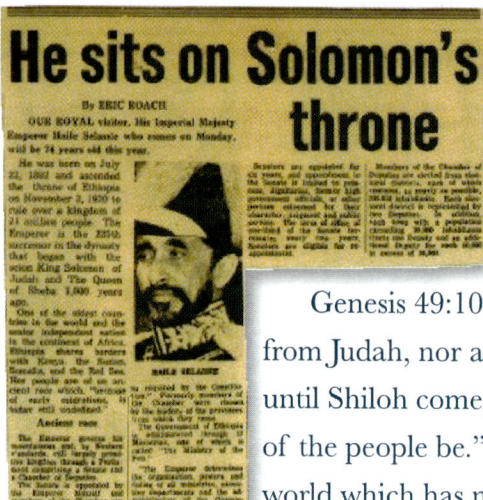

He sits on Solomon's throne

Genesis 49:1 "And Jacob called unto his sons, and said, Gather yourself together, that I may tell you that which shall befall you in the last days."

Genesis 49:10 "The scepter shall not depart from Judah, nor a lawgiver from between his feet, until Shiloh come; and until him shall the gathering of the people be." Ethiopia is the only country in the world which has maintained a direct genealogical family tree of Kings linked to King David.

Germawi Qedamawi Haile Sellassie, is a direct descendent of King David, by way of the union between King Solomon and Queen of Sheba.

Ras Tafari is the 225th in line to King Solomon's dynasty. Hence his title. THE LION OF JUDAH. Germawi Qedamawi Haile Sellassie has fulfilled the biblical scriptures with remarkable style, that is, He is linked to Israel (the Lion of the tribe of Judah) and Ethiopia.

Glory be unto Germawi Qedamawi Haile Sellassie

So as it was in the beginning, so shall it be in the End. Ethiopia in the beginning and Ethiopia in the end.

The prophecies pertaining to Jesus Christ in His second coming are fulfilled by Germawi Qedamawi Haile Sellassie of Ethiopia, and That preciouse name is now revealed.

Ethiopia stretched forth her hands to the Creator (See Psalm 68:31, St John 5:39). Christ said, "You search the Scriptures, for in them you think you have eternal life; and these are they which testify of Me."

2nd Timothy 2:15 "Study to show thyself approved unto God."

Revelation 5:1-8 "And I saw in the right hand of him that sat on the throne a book written within and on the backside, sealed with Seven seals."

And I saw a strong angel proclaiming with a loud voice. Who is worthy to open the book and to loose the seals thereof? And no man in heaven nor on earth, neither under the earth was able to open the book, neither to look thereon. And I wept much because no man was found worthy to open and to read the book, neither to look thereon.

And one of the elders saith unto me. Weep no more. Behold, the Lion of the Tribe of Judah, the Root of David, hath prevailed to open the book and to loose the Seven seals.

"Blessed is he that readeth, and they that hear the words of this prophecy,
and keep those things which are written therein
for the time is at hand."
Revelation 1:3

Revelation 22:13 "I am Alpha and Omega, the beginning and the end, the first and the last."

I in I do give thanks and praise in His precious name,
Germawi Qedamawi Haile Sellassie, Ras Tafari
Ever Living, Ever Faithful, Ever Sure,
King of Kings, Lord of Lords,
The Conquering Lion of The Tribe of Judah,
Elect of God and True Light of the World.
- G. Michael Cordeiro

The War against the King of Kings, the Elect of God

The Italian, Benito Mussolini made war against Germawi Qedamawi Haile Sellassie, and temporarily occupied Ethiopia from May 5th, 1936 to May 5th, 1941. This was a war unlike any that the world had never seen before. The Italian army for the first time in history, "showered" the people of Ethiopia with nerve gas killing all living things under it's rain of terror. During that time of war between Italy and Ethiopia. Germawi Qedamawi Haile Sellassie, stepped on a live bomb and it did not explode.

Isaiah 9: 7 "Of the increase of his government and peace there shall be no end upon the throne of David, and upon his kingdom."

Revelation 17:14 "Those shall make war with the Lamb and the Lamb shall overcome them: for he is Lord of Lords and King of Kings."

Germawi Qedamawi Haile Sellassie on June 10, 1936 appeals to the League of Nations for assistance that had been promised eight months before from the fifty nations when asserted that aggression had been committed in violation of international treaties against his people but was ignored by the same nations.

Therefore, thus fulfilled Isaiah 54:17 "No weapon that is formed against thee shall prosper..."

Daniel 11: 9 "So the king of the south shall come into his kingdom, and shall return into his own land."

Germawi Qedamawi Haile Sellassie, was called Mr. Strong, when he secretly left England to overcome Mussolini's occupation of Ethiopia. He was called Mr. Strong and thus fulfilled Joel 2:11 "And the Lord shall utter his voice before his army: for his camp is very great: for he is Strong that executeth his word".

This was fulfilled because at this time, exactly five years to the day, Germawi Qedamawi Haile Sellassie, the King of Kings and Lord of Lords, defeated Mussolini and regained complete Monarchical Reign.

Durring the military operation to defeat Mussolini, he was called Mr. Smith. This fulfilled Isaiah 54:16. Behold I have created the smith that bloweth the coals in the fire.

It is also worthy to note that after Germawi Qedamawi Haile Sellassie defeated Benito Mussolini, He ordered that no harm be done to the Italian soldiers and sent them all home.

Mussolini was later killed by his own people once the truth was revealed. BBC reported on his death:

"According to the Times correspondent in Milan, the corpses of Mussolini, Petacci and 12 Fascists are on display in Piazzale Loreto with ghastly promiscuity in the open square under the same fence against which one year ago 15 partisans had been shot by their own countrymen".

One woman fired five shots into Mussolini's body, according to Milan Radio, and shouted: "Five shots for my five assassinated sons!" Other passers-by spat on the bodies.

Isaiah 54:16 "Behold, I have created the smith that bloweth the coals in the fire, and that bringeth forth an instrument for his work; and I have created the waster to destroy."

According to this verse, four main themes stand out: the smith, the fire, the coals, and the instrument.

It could be seen that: Germawi Qedamawi Haile Sellassie is the smith, the fire is the waster to destroy, the coals are Benito Mussolini and the other Italians who lost their lives as a result of this war, and the instrument brought forth is His Mighty Name.

It is also worthy to note that Germawi Qedamawi Haile Sellassie was commonly referred to as Mr. Strong as he endlessly fought to regain control of His empire, and that the campaing to sit Him on the throne of King Solomon was the most successful of World War II.

For the reference to the aliases Mr. Strong and Mr. Smith, please see "The Brutality", by A.J. Baler (Ballantine Books Inc.) page 155.

Revelation 3:12 "...Him that overcometh. I will write upon him my new name."

Revelation 19:13 "...His name is called the word of God."

Accolades and Accomplishments

Name: Lij Tafari Mekonnen.

Born: In Ejersa Goro, outside the city of Harrar, Ethiopia on July 23rd, 1892.

Father's name: Ras Wolde Michael Mekonnen.

Mother's name: Wayzero Yishimebet Ali.

Ras Tafari was the ninth of ten children and the only one to survive child birth.

1894 Mother dies from complications of child birth.

1905 Becomes Dejazmatch (Commander or General of the Gate).

1906 Father dies and He becomes governor of Sallale.

1907 Becomes governor of Baso.

1908 Becomes governor of Sidamo.

1910 Becomes governor of Harrar.

1911 Marries Wolete Giorgis (Woizero Menen) of the house of Solomon.

1916 Starts his reign as ruler of Ethiopia.

1917 Officialy becomes a crown Prince.

1918 Abolishes the slave trade in Ethiopia.

1921 Takes his first airplane flight.

1922 Begins to rebuild and modernize Ethiopia.

1923 Ethiopia becomes a member of the League of Nations.

1928 Becomes Negus (King) of Ethiopia.

1930 November 2nd, representatives of 52 nations are witness to the coronation of the King of Kings, Lord of Lords, Conquering Lion of the Tribe of Judah, Emperor of Ethiopia Germawi Qedamawi Haile Sellassie, the elect of God.

1931 Established the first Ethiopian Constitution.

1935 Italy invades Ethiopia by Mussolini's army.

1936 May 2nd H.I.M. Qedamawi Haile Sellassie was forced to exile.

1936 June 10th delivers his historic and prophetic speech to the League of Nations.

1941 May 5th H.I.M. Re-enters Addis Abba with the help of Britain.

1948 Re-established/Redeemed the Ethiopian Orthodox Church from foreign control.

1949 November 7th, H.I.M. lays the foundation for the Qedamawi Haile Sellassie University.

1951 Travels to the Belgrade conference.

1952 February 27th H.I.M. opens College with 150 students.

1952 September 11th H.I.M. ratifies the Ethiopian Constitution.

1954 May 26th Speaks before the United States Congress.

1955 November 2nd Ethiopia celebrates H.I.M.'s Silver Jubilee
    of his coronation.

1958 In December, H.I.M. attends the first conference of
    Independent African States in Accra, Ghana.

1959 Makes his first Official trip to Russia.

1959 H.I.M. creates the Qedamawi Haile Sellassie Foundation.

1959 Receives honourary degree from Charles University,
Czechoslovakia.

1960 May 12th H.I.M. welcomes King Hussein of Jordan
to Ethiopia.

1960 While away visiting Brazil his Imperial Guard forces
attempt a Coup d'état, which is quickly aborted.

1960 On July 17th, H.I.M. Speaks to the African Committee
on Africa today.

1960 Officially opens H.I.M. Airport in Addis Ababa.

1961 Attends the conference of Non Alignment held in Belgrade.

1961 Meets with the members of the Rastafarian community
from Jamaica.

1961 Receives the George Washington Carver Gold Metal Award.

1961 September 3rd H.I.M. addresses the Belgrade Conference.

1962 Empress Menen passes away.

1962 July 12th Speaks at the first graduation of the Qedamawi Haile Sellassie University.

1963 Becomes the founding father of the Organization of African Unity.

1963 September 2nd Visits with President John F Kennedy in Washington.

1963 October 6th H.I.M. addresses the United Nations in New York, USA.

1963 On October 9th, H.I.M. makes His first official visit to Bermuda.

1964 H.I.M. travels to Algeria, Canada, France, Guinea, Mali, Morocco, United States of America, USSR and Tunisia.

1965 On January 21st , H.I.M. formally accepts the title "Defender of the Faith", from an assembly of High Priests (Abbuna) from the Coptic Christian Churches of the world.

1965 On May the 26th, H.I.M. makes a National Broadcast on African Liberation Day.

1965 On November 25th, H.I.M. establishes the first printing press in Ethiopia.

1966 In April, H.I.M. addresses the House of Parliament in Jamaica, and the House of Parliament in Trinidad and Tobago.

1966 In April, H.I.M. visits Porto Prince in Haiti.

1966 Nov. 15 Welcomes the President Antonin Novotney of Czechoslovakia.

His Imperial Majesty, Haile Selassie I In Bermuda—October 9, 1961

The Emperor Haile Selassie I at a tree planting ceremony during his visit to Bermuda, October, 1961. It was said that a church was established in every country the Emperor planted a tree.

1966 Receives the Queen of England Elizabeth II and the Duke of Edinburgh.

1967 February 13th H.I.M. visits with President Lyndon B Johnson of the USA.

1967 February 27 Visits Moscow, USSR.

1967 Makes second visit to Bermuda on route to the Montreal Expo in Canada.

Germawi Qedamawi Haile Sellassie is a founding member of the Organization of African Unity.

31

1969 H.I.M visit's the United States of America and meets with the official dignitaries of the House of Representatives and the House of Senate.

1970 Begins renovating churches in Ethiopia.

1972 Mediates the war between the Sudanese government and the Sudanese rebels.

1973 The United States of America agrees to withdraw from Kagnew. President Gerald Ford signs the edict for the removal of the American presence from Ethiopia.

1974 H.I.M names his grandson Zara Asfa Wossen as heir according to the Ethiopian constitution.

1974 On September the 11th, H.I.M. Qedamawi Haile Sellassie, forced by a military Coup d'état, is formally asked to step down as Emperor. He accepts and is removed from the Monarchy and members of the royal family are placed under arrest.

1975 Germawi Qedamawi Haile Sellassie removes His presence from public view for a time, until He calls a witness unto Himself in 1982 to bear testimony that He lives.

1982 Germawi Qedamawi Haile Sellassie invites the Kriya Yoga Master Yogiraj Sat Gurunath Siddhanath, to a private residence in London, England (in a mansion like home on Great Portland Street) where He was staying as a private and distinguished guest of the Royal Family (See The Chapter: "Meeting the Lion of Judah" from the autobiography of Yogiraj Sat Gurunath Sidhanath: "Wings to Freedom")

All who bear the name of Ras Tafari (Rastafarians) are faithful witnesses of The Father in His Christ, they are One in the same and that Holy Name, The True Ark of the Covenant is revealed unto us all for salvation, redemption, transfiguration unto Ascension.

Germawi Qedamawi Haile Sellassie, lives, rules and reigns for ever and ever, even unto everlasting.

TIME

The Weekly Newsmagazine

"THE KING OF KINGS"

Volume XVI　　　　　　　　　　Number 18

"The King of Kings"

November 3, 1930| Vol. XVI No. 18

34

TIME

The Weekly Newsmagazine

MAN OF THE YEAR

Volume XXVII   Number 1

"Man of the year"
January 6, 1936 | Vol. XXVII No. 1

Medals, Titles and Decorations

The following list of medals was taken from the article Haile Selassie I, The last Emperor by John Duncan McMeekin and is not a complete list.

The Emperor's Foreign Awards

1917   Grand Cordon, The Most Exalted Order of the Queen of Sheba

1923   Military Medal of Merit of the Order of St.George with 3 Palms

1924   Knight Grand Cross, The Imperial Order of Emperor Menelik II

1924   Negus (Knight Grand Cross), The Imperial Order of the Star of Ethiopia

1930   Knight, The Imperial Order of Solomon (no Ribbon)

1930   Knight Grand Cross, The Imperial Order of the Holy Trinity

1930   Coronation Medal of Emperor Haile Sellassie I, 1930

1936   Distinguished Military Medal of Haile Sellassie I, with 3 Palms

1936   Medal for Military Merit in gold

1936   Tigre Expedition Medal in silver, awarded 2 times (2 Palms)

1941   "Dil-Kokeb" The Star of Victory 1941

1941   Medal for Underground Patriotism 1941 with 5 Palms

1944   Medal for Patriotism with 5 Palms

1953   Eritrean Medal of Haile Sellassie I

1955   Imperial Jubilee Coronation Medal

1944   The Refugee's Medal (for war exiles) with 5 palms

1957   Restoration Medal

1959	"Memihiran" Scholarship Medal (also known as Teachers Medal)
1951	Commemorative Medal for the Korean War
1966	25th Anniversaire Medal of the Victory of 1941
1917	U.K. G.C.M.G. (Knight Grand Cross, The Most Distinguished Order of St. Michael & St. George)
1917	Italy, Grand Cross Order of the Crown of Italy (Returned in 1936)
1918	France, Grand Officer, Legion of Honour
1924	Egypt, Grand Cordon, Royal Order of Mohammed Ali
1924	France, Grand Croix, Legion of Honour
1924	Italy, Grand Cross Order of St .Maurice & St. Lazarus (Returned 1936)
1924	Belgium, Grand Cross Order of Leopold (Military Division)
1924	Luxemburg, Knight, Order of the Golden Lion of Nassau
1924	Sweden, Knight, Order of Seraphim
1924	U.K. G.C.B., (Knight Grand Cross, Most Honourable Order of the Bath)
1924	Portugal, Grand Cross Military Order of Aviz
1924	Greece, Grand Cross Royal Order of the Redeemer
1925	Portugal, Grand Cross Military Order of the Tower & Sword
1928	Italy, Knight, Supreme Order of the Annunciation (Returned 1936)
1930	Egypt, Collar, Royal Order of Mohammed Ali
1930	Netherlands, Grand Cross Civil Order of Merit of the Netherlands Lion
1930	Poland, Grand Cross Order of Polonia Restituta
1930	Japan, Grand Commander, Supreme Order of the Chrysanthemum
1930	U.K. G.C.V.O. (Knight Grand Cross, Royal Victorian Order)
1930	U.K. The Royal Victorian Chain
1945	USA, Chief Commander, Legion of Merit
1945	Norway Grand Cross with Collar, Order of St. Olav
1949	Finland, Grand Cross with Collar, Order of the White Rose
1949	Portugal, Ribband of the Three Orders
1949	Spain, Grand Cross with Collar, Distinguished Order of Charles III
1950	Lebanon, Superior Class, The Merit Decoration
1950	Syria, Grand Cordon, Order of Omayyadh
1950	Jordan, Grand Commander, Order of Hussein Ibn Ali (no Sash ?)
1950	Iraq, Grand Cordon with Collar, Order of the Hashemites
1953	U.K. Coronation Medal 1953
1954	Mexico, Grand Collar, Order of the Aztec Eagle
1954	Yugoslavia, The Yugoslav Grand Star
1954	Czechoslovakia, 1st Class with Collar, Order of the White Lion
1954	Austria, Grand Decoration of Honour in Gold with Sash, Decoration of Honour for Merit

1954	Germany, Gran Cross Special Class, Order of Merit of the Federal Republic of Germany
1954	France, Croix de Guerre with Palm (War Cross)
1954	France, Medaille Militaire (Military Medal)
1954	U.K., K.G. (Knight, Noble Order of the Garter) (No Sash or Ribbon)
1954	Netherlands, Grand Cross Military Order of Willem (William)
1954	Denmark, Knight, Order of the Elephant
1954	Sweden, Collar, Order of Seraphim (no Sash)
1955	Italy, Grand Cross with Collar, Order of Merit of the Italian Republic
1956	Libya, Grand Collar, Royal Order of Idris I
1956	Japan, Collar, Supreme Order of the Chrysanthemum
1956	Republic of Korea (South Korea), 1st Class, Order of National Foundation
1958	Brazil, GC with Collar, Order of the Southern Cross
1958	Pakistan, 2nd Class, Order of Pakistan (Hilal-i-Pakistan)
1958	Burma Grand Commander, Agha Maha Thudhamma
1958	Thailand, Knight, Most Illustrious Order of the Royal House of Chakri
1958	Malaysia, Grand Knight, Most Exalted Order of the National Crown
1958	Indonesia, 1st Class, Bintang Republik Indonesia
1958	Vietnam 1st Class, National Order of Vietnam
1958	Philippines, Raja, Ancient Order of Sikatuna
1960	Somalia, Grand Cordon, Order of the Somali Star
1963	Togo, Grand Commander, Order of Mono
1963	Upper Volta, Grand Cordon, National Order of Upper Volta
1963	Ivory Coast, Grand Cross National Order of Cote d?Ivoire
1963	Liberia, Knight Grand Band, Order of the Pioneers of the Republic
1963	Senegal, Grand Cross Order of the Lion
1963	Mali, Grand Cross with Collar, National Order of Merit
1963	Niger, Grand Cross National Order of Niger
1963	Chad, Grand Cross National Order of Merit
1963	Nigeria, Grand Commander, Order of the Federal Republic
1964	Hungary, 1st Class with Diamonds, Order of the Banner of the P.R. of Hungary (no Ribbon)
1964	Tunisia, Grand Collar, Order of Independence
1962	Morocco, Grand Collar, Order of Mohammed (no Ribbon)
1964	Buganda, Commander, Order of the Shield & Spears of Buganda Kingdom
1964	Iran, Collar, Pahlevi Order of Iran
1966	Dahomey, CC National Order of Dahomey
1966	Cambodia, Grand Collar, Order of Independence
1966	Haiti, Grand Cross Order of Honour & Merit

1966	Venezuela Grand Cross with Collar, The Order of the Bust of the Liberator Simon Bolivar
1966	Bolivia, Grand Cross National Order of the Condor of the Andes
1966	Peru, Grand Cross Order of the Peruvian Sun
1966	Chile, Grand Cross with Collar, Order of Merit
1966	Kenya, Grand Chief, Order of the Golden Heart
1967	Iran, Coronation Medal of the Shah of Iran 1967

1968/70	Zaire, Grand Cross with Collar, Order of the Leopard
1968/70	Burundi, Grand Cross Order of the Republic
1968/70	Malawi, Grand Cross Order of the Lion
1968/70	Zambia, Grand Commander, Order of the Eagle of Zambia
1968 /70	Malagasy Republic, Grand Commander, National Order of the Malagasy Republic
1968/70	Central African Republic, Grand Cross Order of Merit of Central Africa
1968/70	Congo, Grand Cross National Order of Congolese Merit
1968/70	Gabon, Grand Commander, Order of the Equatorial Star
1968/70	Cameroun, Grand Cross Order of Valour
1968/70	Mauritania, Grand Cordon, National Order of Mauritania
1968/70	Guinea, Grand Cordon, National Order of Guinea

1970	Sudan, The Insignia of Honour
1970	Vatican State, Knight Grand Cross, Order of Pius IX
1970	Ghana, 1st Class, Order of the Star
1970	Argentina Grand Cross Order of San Martin
1970	Iraq 1st Class, Order of Ar-Rafidan (Military Division)
1971	Iran, 2500 Anniversaire Medal of the Foundation of the Persian Monarchy
1971	Saudi Arabia, Grand Cordon, Order of King Abdul Aziz
1972	Uganda, Grand Commander, Order of the Source of the Nile

Utterances of His Imperial Majesty

H.I.M. addresses the Unted Nations

Today, I stand before the world organization which has succeeded to the mantle discarded by its discredited predecessor. In this body is enshrined the principle of collective security which I unsuccessfully invoked at Geneva. Here, in this Assembly, reposes the best - perhaps the last - hope for the peaceful survival of mankind.

In 1936, I declared that it was not the Covenant of the League that was at stake, but international morality. Undertakings, I said then, are of little worth if the will to keep them is lacking. The Charter of the United Nations expresses the noblest aspirations of man: abjuration of force in the settlement of disputes between states; the assurance of human rights and fundamental freedoms for all without distinction as to race, sex, language or religion; the safeguarding of international peace and security.

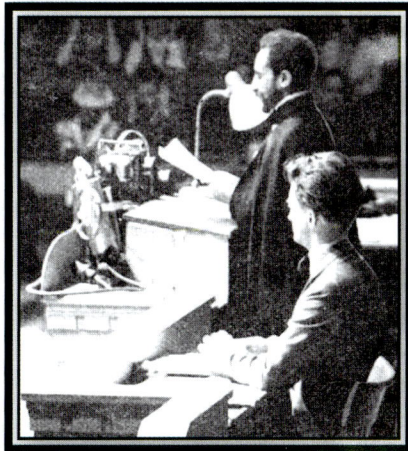

United Nations October 1963

... Until the philosophy which holds one race superior and another inferior is finally and permanently discredited and abandoned: That until there are no longer first-class and second class citizens of any nation; That until the color of a man's skin is of no more significance than the color of his eyes; That until the basic human Rights are equally guaranteed to all without regard to race; That until that day, the dream of lasting peace and world citizenship and rule of international morality will remain but a fleeting illusion, to be pursued but never attained; And until the ignoble and unhappy regimes that hold our brothers in Angola, in Mozambique and in South Africa in subhuman bondage have been toppled and destroyed; Until bigotry and prejudice and malicious and inhuman self-interest have been replaced by understanding and tolerance and good-will; Until all Africans stand and speak as free beings, equal in the eyes of all men, as they are in the eyes of Heaven; Until that day, the African continent will not know peace. We Africans will fight, if necessary, and we know that we shall win, as we are confident in the victory of good over evil."

Equality of representation must be assured in each of its organs. The possibilities which exist in the United Nations to provide the medium whereby the hungry may be fed, the naked clothed, the ignorant instructed, must be seized on and exploited for the flower of peace is not sustained by poverty and want. To achieve this requires courage and confidence. The courage, I believe, we possess. The confidence must be created, and to create confidence we must act courageously.

- Germawi Qedamawi Haile Sellassie

... When I spoke at Geneva in 1936, there was no precedent for a head of state addressing the League of Nations. I am neither the first, nor will I be the last head of state to address the United Nations, but only I have addressed both the League and this Organization in this capacity. The problems which confront us today are, equally, unprecedented. They have no counterparts in human experience. Men search the pages of history for solutions, for precedents, but there are none.

This, then, is the ultimate challenge. Where are we to look for our survival, for the answers to the questions which have never before been posed? We must look, first, to Almighty God, Who has raised man above the animals and endowed him with intelligence and reason. We must put our faith in Him, that He will not desert us or permit us to destroy humanity which He created in His image. And we must look into ourselves, into the depth of our souls. We must become something we have never been and for which our education and experience and environment have ill-prepared us. We must become bigger than we have been: more courageous, greater in spirit, larger in outlook. We must become members of a new race, overcoming petty prejudice, owing our ultimate allegiance not to nations but to our fellow men within the human community.

- Germawi Qedamawi Haile Sellassie

H.I.M. speaks on the Bible

We in Ethiopia have one of the oldest versions of the Bible, but however old the version may be, in whatever language it might be written, the word remains one and the same. It transcends all boundaries of empires and all conceptions of race. It is eternal. No doubt you all remember reading in the Act of the Apostles how Philip baptized the Ethiopian official. He is the first Ethiopian on record to have followed Christ and from that day onwards the Word of God has continued to grow in the hearts of Ethiopians. And I might say for myself that from early childhood I was taught to appreciate the Bible and my love for it increases with the passage of time. All through my troubles I have found it a cause of infinite comfort "Come unto Me", all ye that labour and are heavy laden and I will give you rest, Who can resist an invitation so full of compassion? Because of this personal experience in the goodness of the Bible. I was resolved that all my countrymen should also share its great blessings and that by reading the Bible they should find truth for themselves.

Therefore, I caused a new translation to be made from our ancient language into the language which the old and the young understood and spoke. Today man sees all his hopes and aspirations crumbling before him. He is perplexed and knows not whither he is drifting. But he must realize that the Bible is his refuge and the rallying point for all humanity. In it, man will find the solution of his present difficulties and guidance for his future action and unless he accepts with clear conscience the Bible and its great Message, he cannot hope for salvation. For my part I glory in the Bible.

- Germawi Qedamawi Haile Sellassie

H.I.M. speaks on spirituality

The temple of the most high begins with the human body, which houses our life, essence of our existence. Africans are in bondage today because they approach spirituality through Religion provided by foreign invaders and conquerors. We must stop confusing religion and spirituality. Religion is a set of rules, regulations and rituals created by humans which were supposed to help people grow spiritually.

Due to human imperfection religion has become corrupt, political, divisive and a tool for power struggle. Spirituality is not theology or ideology. It is simply a way of life, pure and original as was given by the Most High. Spirituality is a network linking us to the Most High, the universe and each other. As the essence of our existence it embodies our culture, true identity, nationhood and destiny.

A people without a nation they can really call their own is a people without a soul. Africa is our nation and is in spiritual and physical bondage because her leaders are turning to outside forces for solutions to African problems when everything Africa needs is within her. When African righteous people come together, the world will come together. This is our divine destiny.

- Germawi Qedamawi Haile Sellassie

Tribes of Israel

The following is a depiction of the flags belonging to the twelve tribes of Israel.

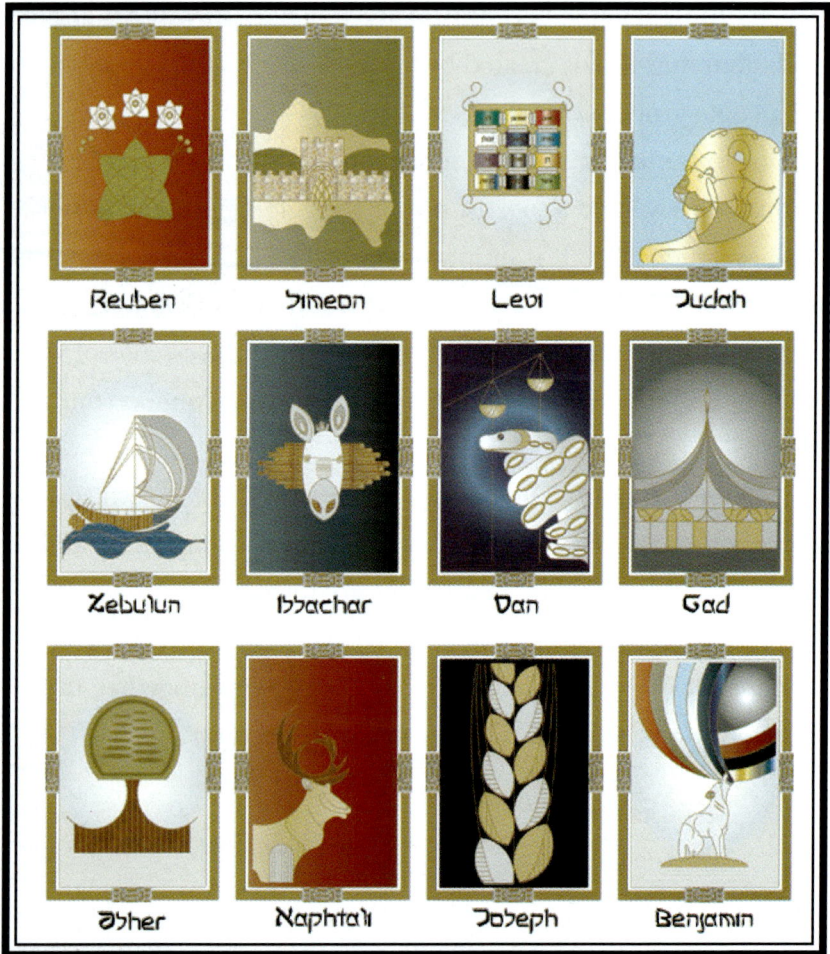

Reuben	Simeon	Levi	Judah
Zebulun	Issachar	Dan	Gad
Asher	Naphtali	Joseph	Benjamin

Other Important Figures

Marcus Garvey

In the early 19th century Marcus Garvey said for all Africans to "Look to the east for the coronation of an African King."

Therefore, he prophesied that The Almighty would send a Divine Ruler (Son of Man) to rule Ethiopia, thus fulfilling: Psalms 87:4 "...this man was born there."

Robert Nesta Marley

"How long shall they kill our prophets, while we stand aside and look. Some say it's just apart of it, we've got to fulfill the book."

"Give us the teachings of His Majesty, For we no want no devil philosophy."

The Father's Prayer in Ge'ez, Amharic and English

ጸሎት::
TSA-LOT
Prayer

አባታችን:ሆይ=በሰማይ:የምትኖር፡
ABBA-TA-CHIN HOY   BESEM-MAY   YEMIT-NOR
Oh Our FATHER   In Heaven   Who Lives

ስምህ:ይቀደስ:መንግሥትህ:ትምጣ::
SIM-MIH   YIQ-QEDES   MEN-GISH-TIH   TIM-TTÁ
Your Name   Is Holy   Your Rulership   Is To Come

ፈቃድህ:በሰማይ:እንደሆነች÷
FEQ-QAAD-DIH   BESEM-MAY   INDE-HONECH
Your Will   In Heaven   Like, As She Became

እንዲሁ:በምድር:ትሁን::
IN-DEE-HU   BEM-MIDIR   TI-HUN
Like This   In Earth   To Be

የዕለት:እንጀራችንን:ስጠን:ዛሬ:
YE'IL-LET   IN-JERA-CHININ   SITTEN   ZA-REY
Of Day: Daily   Our Bread   Give US   To Day

በደላችንንም:ይቅር:በለን፡ እኛ:
BEDELA-CHIN-NIM   YIQ-QIR   BEL-LEN   IN-NAA
Our Wrongdoings   Excuse, Forgive   For Us   We

የበደሉንን:ይቅር:እንደምንል::
YEBEDEL-LUNIN   YIQ-QIR   INDE-MINIL
They Who Wrong Us   Excuse   Like, As We

ወደ ፈተ ንም:አታግባን፡
WEDE-FETEN-NAM   AT-TAAG-BAAN
Towards Temptation   We Will Not Enter

ከክፉ : አድነን:እንጂ::
KE-KIF-FU   ADIN-NIN   IN-JEE
From the Evil   We Are Saved   On the Other Hand/But

መንግሥት:ያንተ:ናትና::
MEN-GISHT   YANTE   NAT-TIN-NA
the Rulership   Yours   For She Is

ሃይልም:ምስጋናም:ለዘለዓለሙ::
HAY-YILIM   MIS-GAAN-NAAM   LEZELE-AALEM-MU
And Power   And Thanks/Praise   Are Forever/World
Without End

አሜን::
AM-MEYN
The True And Faithfull Witness

The Father's Prayer in Amharic

The Father's Prayer In English

Bessim Ab	*In the name of The Father,*
WeWolde We Menfes	*The Son, and The Holy-Spirit, One*
Qidus Ahadu Amlak	*living Creator*
Selah	*(Pause for reverence)*
Kibure le:	*Glory be unto:*
Germawi	*His Imperial Majesty*
Qedamawi Haile Sellassie	*Haile Sellassie 1st*
Abatachin Hoy Besemay Yemitnor	*Our Father which art in Heaven*
Simmeh Yekedes	*Hallowed be thy name.*
Mengistih Timta	*Thy Kingdom come*
Indehum Bemedir Tihun	*Thy will is done on Earth*
Fekadeh Besemay Indehonech	*As it is in Heaven*
Yeilet Injerachinin Siten Zare	*Give us this day our daily bread*
Bedelachininim Yeker Belen	*And forgive us our debts,*
Enyam Yebedelu Yeker Endeminil	*as we forgive our debtors*
Abetu Wede Fetenan Atagban	*And lead us not to temptation but*
Kekifu adimnin injee	*deliver us from evil,*
Mengist Yante Natinna	*For the kingdom, She is yours,*
Haylim Kibre Misganna	*And the power, and the glory,*
Lezelamu	*forever*
Selah	*(Pause for reverance)*

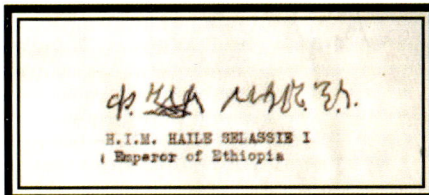

H.I.M. HAILE SELASSIE I
Emperor of Ethiopia

49

Psalms 23
A Psalm of David

The Lord is my shepherd, I shall not Want.
He maketh me to lie in green pastures,
He leadeth me besides the still waters.
He restoreth my soul,
He leadeth me in The path of righteousness
For his name's Sake.
Yea, though I walk through the valley
Of the shadow of death.
I will fear no evil, For thou art with me,
thy rod and thy staff, they comfort me.
Thou prepares a table before me
in The presence of my enemies,
thou anointest my head with oil,
my cup runneth over.
Surely goodness and mercy shall follow Me
All the days of my life and I will dwell
In the house of the Lord for ever.

Dedicated to my Earthly Father:

John Alexander Cordeiro
1920 - 2001

O' Father,

Ras Tafari, Germawi Qedamawi Haile Sellassie

Ever living, Ever faithful, Ever sure,

The Holy One of Israel,

The Ancient of days,

The Son of Man,

The Second Adam,

The Prince of Peace,

Conquering Lion of the tribe of Judah

And true light of the World

Have mercy on I-in-I O' Lord Almighty

Guide and protect us-all

And lead I-in-I upon the path of up-righteousness

and through the trials and tribulations of life

Yes O' Mighty Father

Ever living, Ever faithful, Ever sure

Germawi Qedamawi Haile Sellassie,

Most High Ras Tafari

Emperor Haile Sellassie the First.

Seek ye the Kingdom of God first

For all it's Glory and Righteousness

And all things will be given unto you after.

- G Michael Cordeiro

John 3: 16 "For GOD so loveth the world, that he gave his only begotten Son, that Who so ever believeth in him should not perish, but have everlasting Life..."

Proverbs 1: 7 "The fear of the Lord is the beginning Of knowledge; but fools despise Wisdom and instruction..."

"Let the words of my mouth and the meditations of my heart be acceptable in thy sight."

In Memory Of:

Michael C. Dias
Jan. 1976 – June 2001

Glen O'Brian
Sept. 1963 – Feb. 1997

Dennis De Silva
July 1963 – May 2009

Donahue H. Sousa Sr.
Nov. 1963 Jan 2009

Bibliography

1: The Holy Bible. King James version.
2: Visions of Rastafari. By Lance Seunarine.
3: Haile Sellassie And The Opening Of Seven Seals. By
Kalin Ray Salassie. Research Associates.
4: The KEBRA NAGAST The lost Bible of Rastafarian
Wisdom and Faith from Ethiopia and Jamaica. By Gerald
Hausman, intro by Ziggy Marley
5: The Rastafari IBLE. The Books Of
    1. The Glory Of Kings
    2. The Utterance Of Jah By Jahson Atiba Alemu I
6. The Holy Piby. By Shepherd Robert Athlyi Rogers, intro by
Miguel Lorne, forward by Ras Sekou Tafari.
7: The Autobiography of Haile Sellassie I vol. II. Research
Associates.
8: Haile Sellassie I in Bermuda 1963 & 1967. By Dale Butler
The Writers Machine.
9: JAHUG - Vol. 1 Edition 2. By C. Gayle & T. Gayle for
Repatriation Productions.
10: Haile Sellassie: The Conguering Lion Of The Tribe Of
Judah. By Brian K. Buckner.
11: Dictionary of Gods and Goddesses Devils and Demons. By
Manfred Lurker, page 113, for referrence to Ess.
12: Webster's Third New International Dictionary, page 61, for
the Hebrew alphabet.
13: Unger's Bible Dictionary, page 301, for Elias.
14: Unger's Bible Dictionary, page 327, for referrence to Ethiopia.
15: Unger's Bible Dictionary, page 231, for referrence to Cush.
16: Medals and Decorations, Article "Haile Selassie, The Last
Emperor: http://www.docstoc.com/docs/51504291/HAILE-
SELASSIE-1-The-Last-Emperor
17: Flages of the Twelve Tribes of Israel: http://annamars-
zalkowska.com/blog/?q=twelve-tribes-of-Israel

Glossary

Tri-unity:
It is important also to note the differences between the words and concepts behind the words Tri-Unity and Trinity. Tri-Unity means one person (physically or spiritually). Contrarily, Trinity means three persons. (John 14:11) Christ said to Phillip: "...He that hath seen me hath seen the Father. I am in the Father and the Father in me. Believe me that I am in the Father and the Father in me" Phillip was looking at one person. Christ one physical fleshy person like your Father.

I-in-I:
Refers to the "I-ness" within "I", the sense of self, or self-awareness, which is of the soul. It is a way of saying, I, the conscious witnessor. This is similar to the meaning of the Sanskrit word Manaste, which essentialy means: the awareness in me, is acknowleding the awareness in you... or I-in-I sight the I in the I.

Rastafarian:
Refers to any man or woman who bares witness to Ras Tafari Mekonnen as the Holy Elect One, The Christ in His second advent, Germawi Qedamawi Haile Sellassie (His Imperial Majest Haile Sellassie the First).

H.I.M.
Ras Tafari

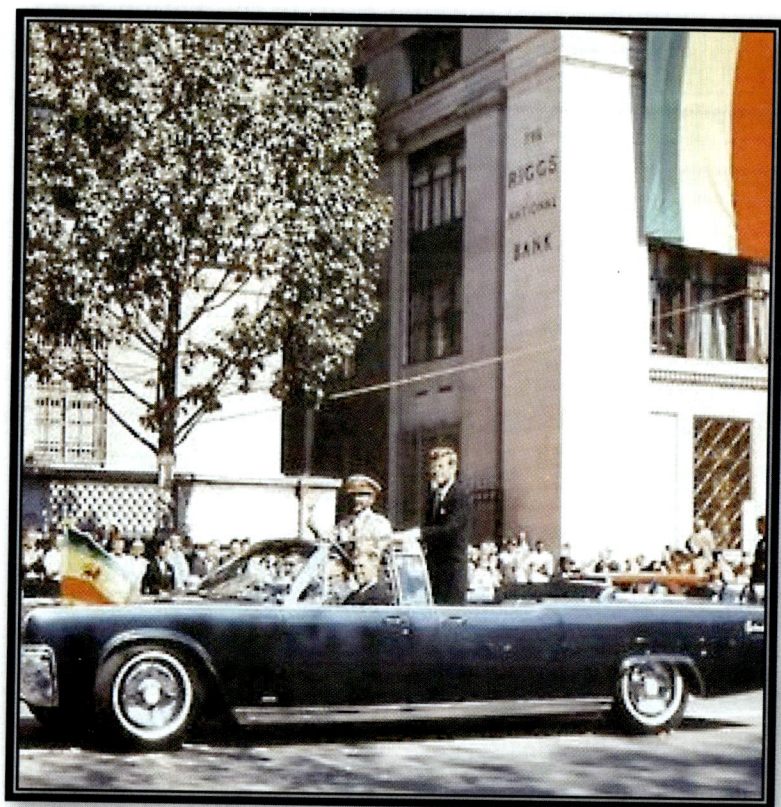

The Conquering Lion
of the Tribe of Judah

Omega.